A Collection of Children's Books

The Soft Stories
The Night I Was Scared
and
Look at Me

Ketly Pierre

To order additional copies of this book, contact:
Xlibris
1-888-795-4274
www.Xlibris.com
Orders@Xlibris.com

Love to my families, friends, and readers.

First and foremost, I give thanks to my Lord and Savior for blessing me with this opportunity to write **A Collection of Children's Books.**

Book 1

The Soft Book

Story and Photographs by
Ketly Pierre

See my bows? How soft is it? Is it soft to place in your hair? Is it soft to touch with your fingers?

Yes, it is soft.

See my flowers? How soft is it? Is it soft to touch with your fingers? Is it soft to put in your hair?

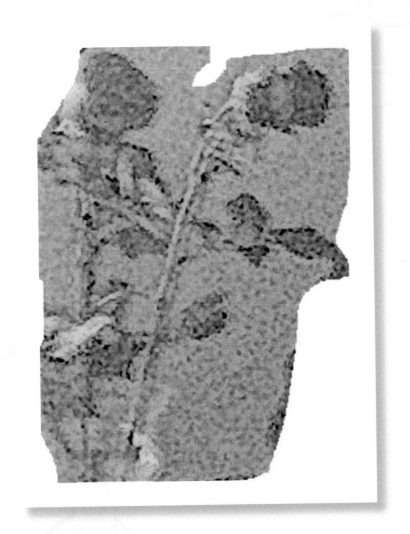

Yes, it is soft.

See my teddy bear? How soft is it? Is it soft to hold in your hand? And is it soft enough to make you feel happy?

Yes, it is soft.

See my **blanket**? How soft is it? Is it soft to sit on? Is it soft to wrap around your body? Is it soft to touch to your cheek?

Yes, it is soft.

See my rug? How soft is it? Is it soft for you to sit on? Is it soft for you to walk on without any shoes?

Yes, it is soft.

See my baby? How soft is my baby? Is my baby soft when hugged? Is my baby soft when kissed on the forehead?

Place your baby's picture here.
Yes, you are soft.

Book 2

The Night I Was Scared

Written and Illustrated by

Ketly Pierre

One day, there was little girl name Linda-lee who heard a squeaky sound early in the morning. Squeak screech, she heard, as if it were a ghost moaning out of pain. In that moment, she sat up in bed, trying to be brave, to see where that noise was coming from. Squeak screech! Linda-lee heard again as her eyes wandered throughout the dim bedroom. Then her fear kicked in, and her braveness kicked out. Her heart beat loudly like a drum to see, standing next to the drawer, a shadow of a ghost. Linda-lee gasped, trying to breathe and to pick her jaw off the floor.

Immediately, her heart raced more out of control, as if she were running a marathon. Her hands became numb as if it were frozen cold. And in the midst of it all, Linda-lee found herself holding on to the comforter close to her face, just enough to see with her teary eyes. And underneath the comforter, Linda-lee's knees were bent close to her body, losing all her ability to control her voice and her body's movement, except the movement of her eyes as it moved from side to side.

Squeak screech! The noise got louder and louder. And in that moment, Linda-lee found the ability to unfreeze her voice. She screamed at the top of her lungs, running out of the bedroom door as if she had four legs. Without any anticipation of how scared she really was, Linda-lee tripped and lay on top, her dog, Jackie. It was then that she remembered her dog was sleeping in front of the bedroom door, snoring so loudly with that squeaking sound of a ghost. She gasped and then laughed out loud. "It was not a ghost after all," Linda-lee said.

"Oh, my dog and my imagination, with that squeaking sound like the noise of a ghost. This has been a night I was scared over a shadow of a ghost." Within moments, she fell fast asleep. Good night to you all.

BOOK 3
LOOK AT ME

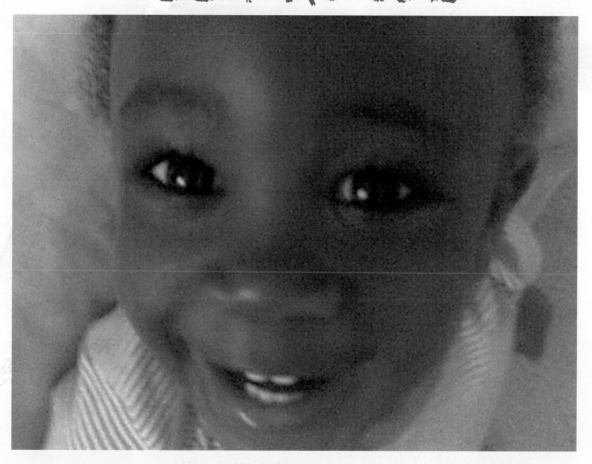

WRITTEN AND ILLUSTRATED BY
KETLY PIERRE

I AM GROWING UP. LOOK AT ME.
I AM WALKING ALL BY MYSELF.

I AM GROWING UP. LOOK AT ME.

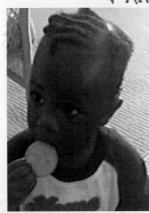

I AM EATING ALL BY MYSELF.

I AM GROWING UP. LOOK AT ME.
I AM CLIMBING THE STAIRS ALL BY MYSELF.

I AM GROWING UP. LOOK AT ME.
I AM CLIMBING UP THE ROCK MOUNTAIN ALL BY
MYSELF.

I AM GROWING UP. LOOK AT ME.
I AM PLAYING THE PIANO ALL BY MYSELF. AND I CAN
PLAY THE PIANO WITH MY SISTER TOO.

LOOK AT ME. I AM ALL GROWN-UP NOW. WOW!
I AM ONE YEAR OLD NOW.

Printed in the United States
By Bookmasters